SUGAR

Also by Andrea Cohen

The Cartographer's Vacation

Long Division

Kentucky Derby

Furs Not Mine

Unfathoming

Nightshade

Everything

The Sorrow Apartments

SUGAR

Andrea Cohen

Four Way Books
Tribeca

for

now

and

then

and

when

I made a snowman and my brother knocked it down and I knocked my brother down and then we had tea.

—Dylan Thomas

Library of Congress Cataloging-in-Publication Data

Names: Cohen, Andrea, 1961- author
Title: Sugar / Andrea Cohen.
Other titles: Sugar (Compilation)
Description: Tribeca : Four Way Books, 2026.
Identifiers: LCCN 2025027283 (print) | LCCN 2025027284 (ebook) | ISBN 9781961897700 trade paperback | ISBN 9781961897717 ebook
Subjects: LCGFT: Poetry
Classification: LCC PS3603.O3415 S84 2026 (print) | LCC PS3603.O3415 (ebook)
LC record available at https://lccn.loc.gov/2025027283
LC ebook record available at https://lccn.loc.gov/2025027284

This book is manufactured in the United States of America and printed on acid-free paper.

Four Way Books is a not-for-profit literary press. We are grateful for the assistance we receive from individual donors, public arts agencies, and private foundations including the New York State Council on the Arts, a state agency.

NEW YORK STATE OF OPPORTUNITY. Council on the Arts

PROUD MEMBER
[clmp]

We are a proud member of the Community of Literary Magazines and Presses.

Contents

Matinée

Today the part
of love will be played

by regret. Memory
will be played

by what if, tragedy
by the saxophonist.

Silence will be played
by silence. There will be

no intermission.

I

Losing My Religion

The truth is I left it on the bus
on purpose. Because I saw someone

else's religion there and didn't
want it to be lonely. The truth

is you should never begin
anything with *the truth is*

because then people will think
everything else you were saying

was false. The truth is all
I wanted was this: to fall

asleep with you at the bus
station, still holding our coffee

cups, still holding our scepters.

Hem

My first address
was a dress—

a hem I held
onto. Every

house since
has been

a tenement—
flimsy

and temporary.

Spectacle

On sad days we'd go
to the planetarium.

We'd put on that
helmet of stars

and hardly anything
falling could hurt us.

Habitat

The gods ran
back and forth

between
our houses—

like those dogs
who pretend

no one
has fed them.

Track and Field

I was big so they had
me throw things—

discus, javelin, shotput.
They taught me how

to hop and run and
spin with an object I

held tight and then
let fly. It was like

seeing a heaviness
in me grow wings—

and then, always,
a small man, scurrying,

would take my measure.

Safe

It's bolted to the floor
of my childhood,
in the basement
cedar closet—
a locked room
in a locked room
where my mother
keeps the shimmering
bits of herself
in velvet pouches,
in tissue and
laminated boxes
and when it's her
turn to get a shiny
diagnosis, we go
down there. It's
a warm summer
morning and we sit
cross-legged, like
children on the floor,
and the power's
out, so I'm holding
a flashlight while
my mother turns

the dial, aligning
the tumblers. We're
trying to be quiet
because my father
is in the next room
listening to patients
trying to fix themselves
via time travel. The closet
smells like a forest, and
inside the evergreens
my mother asks: *This,*
this, this? Because I've
asked for something,
some brightness she
can hand off before
the avalanche of every-
thing without her.
And suddenly my father
has pushed the door open.
He's standing there with
a paperweight the drug
company gave him, with
his boy scout flashlight,
thinking *thieves*, thinking

his job is to keep us
safe—and there we are,
laps glitter-filled, breaking
into our beautiful, fugitive
lives.

Bell

It was a small
dinner bell. It

was silver and
she rang it

whenever she
was hungry

for the memory
of someone coming.

Cookies

after Razia Iqbal

I ate so
many cookies—

madeleines—
at the wake.

I was trying
to recall

what hunger
must taste like.

My Father's Watch

It's a Bulova, nothing fancy.
It sits in his desk, then in mine.

Finally, I take it to Leo, who
does what I never thought to do.

He winds it. He lifts it to my ear.
It won't keep perfect time, he says—

which is fine. Time is imperfect.
It soldiers on, we say, as if

it wasn't us sabering
the days and nights.

Trees on the path.
Rain on the leaves.

This ticking along—
I miss him.

Musical Chairs

The chairs don't actually
sing or play instruments.

The soundtrack is always
prerecorded. It always sounds

like this: *keep running, keep running,*
a little tinny and singsongy,

and then it stops and some-
one gasps and someone

whose lap you began
in has vanished.

Onions

I always think of Pauline going
down the stairs I always hold
on thinking how going down
she must have tripped she
was always going fast after
all we called her The Flash
and when her husband
found her it didn't matter
that he was an ER doc he
might as well have been a post-
doc in art history he might as
well have been a window
washer or mortician there
she was at the bottom
of the stairs with that busted
sack of onions sweet onions
she'd have sliced and cried
over and eaten raw with a little
salt and she'd have handed
you a slice like a sliver
of moon and if you
were in a dark
time she'd have
said hey friend hold
on

Those Red Hills

Where I come from,
a hunting accident

is what we called
it when a boy

went into the woods
with a gun, when

someone hauled
his body back,

having buried
the gun, so no

other boy could
do anything

but mourn it.

Song

Here, here,
the bird sings,

and if only I
could get there,

it wouldn't sound
like every dirge

I've ever heard.

Wax

A ball of wax
is the whole
ball of wax,
no matter
how small,
no matter
how soft
or hard,
or how
many
rooms
it fills
or fails
with
light
to fill.

Piecemeal

One black crow
          flying through

this blue day—
          all jagged, all

edges—like one
          piece of a jigsaw

in search
                    of a puzzle.

Sugar

What was the name of that
bar was it really the Sugar
Club is it still there who were
we with running in from the cold
and wind and you could still
smoke in bars then you could
still go home with six cartons
of smoke in your hair we all
had hair for days then our
hands got lost in it and our faces
and how crowded the bar was
and hot too and I liked running and
being useful and you and ran back
to the blue Chevy Nova to stash
our coats in the trunk and ran
back and "Lush Life" was playing
and Bowie and yelling to be
heard and the lights in the bar
flashing because that part
of the night was ending and out
we went to the street it was Hoboken
it was 1983 right before Christmas
and I turned left and everybody
else went in the other direction and

this way you said and I said no
no I ought to know I'm the one
who ran back to the car with all
our coats and the key and who
could have guessed what are
the odds that it was somebody
else's car our key unlocked and
that blue Nova was long gone
to Teaneck or Long Branch or
Secaucus and we looked and
looked in the empty dark of our
car's trunk it was like looking
for gold at the 7-Eleven and
someone said how stupid could
you be and it wasn't a question and
one of us couldn't stop crying knowing
someone had her yellow coat and
maybe her whole life to come and
what are the odds forty summers
later here we are on a hilltop in Italy
and you tell the story but in this
version it's you and your pals
from high school in Maplewood
Joey and Emma and Gabe and

what's-his-name and as it happens it
happened before I ever knew you
you say so I was never there
and the name of the place
was Sugar Reef on Second Avenue
in the city not in Hoboken and
down there in the dusk of the valley
lights are coming on and above
us swallows and clouds like
threads from a jacket unraveling
and from some hidden speaker
Lady Day is singing *Sugar*
I never maybe my sugar—
maybe as an action item—
imagine—and if I never was
here please please don't tell me

II

Bees in Winter

They buzz
more loudly

in flowers
recalled.

Ghosting

How cavalier
people are—

with language
and with silence.

Any ghost will
tell you—

the last thing
we mean

to do
is leave you.

Shepherd

Without my
sheep I'd
be lost.

Design Flaw

Holding awe
in check.

On Desire

A part of me
wants

to be
all of me.

Poker Face

Mine won't say
my favorite
game is solitaire.

Dusk

The sun
has gone

to another
party without us.

Into the Light

Reckless, daredevil
moths—they've

even chewed
through their flight plan.

Breaking News

We were al-
ready broken.

Clarity

The crystal glass
flung shatters

the evening
you thought

crystal
clear isn't

Proximity

She died
of my wounds.

Stretch

I'll see you
in heaven, we

say, making
ends meet.

Introduction to Color

It

fades.

Heavy Lifting

On the huge

blue dumpster—

trash/basuro.

Why not,

on high—

cielo/sky?

Unbearable

What does
it look like?

Like
any cub

on any
bear rug.

Collateral Damage

Language can
only do so

much—partial
remains remain

a total loss.

Independence Day, Arezzo

If you were
here, I could

say why
I love you

and good
riddance

without
a stamp.

Trail Running

The trail
ran one

way—I
ran another.

Contingency

for Razia

In another
life I'd
want this one.

Batting Cages

If only
the boys

with bats
would stay

in their cages.

Heaven

It's hell
for the girls

who loved
bad boys.

Keepsake

She gave
me nothing—
nothing lasts.

Selfie Stick

I'd rather

have a carrot.

Bio

Andrea Cohen
is and will
be was.

Kettle Pond

after Basho

Another frog
jumps in—

water
applauds.

Brief History of the Cosmos

Wattage
costs—

darkness
comes

free
of charge.

Directional

He held
a match

up
to see

which way
the dark

was headed.

Clover

She hovered
above her life—

like a bee
who'd forgotten

what flowers
are for.

III

On Love

You can't climb
on top and call

yourself conqueror,
or straddling, whip

love into submission.
Love wanders from sky

to sky—once or twice
I've seen it there

or felt a presence
other than my own—

a kind of glowing
twilight makes

before it tires
of one place.

Fruitless

Who said
fruit
was the point

of it all?
All
I wanted

was to stand
in a field
near your branches.

Sentences

The saddest two?
I wish I'd

kissed you then,
and the distant

runner-up—*I*
wish I didn't.

Tunnel

Never an Everest
of love. Always
a tunnel. Never
a ride they sink
much money
into, but a slap-
dash fiasco,
a dimly lit fire
hazard as likely
to showcase fan-
blown ghosts as
plaster cupids. You
know the drill: they
strap you into
the two-person
boat attached
to a rusty track
and off you go
for the six-
minute lurch
through the cross
between haunted
house and Okefenokee.
Six minutes to

neck and unzip,
six minutes to be
oblivious to the flashing
red eyes of would-
be crocodiles
in fetid water, six
minutes to kiss
and fumble and
whatever else
is allowed two
bodies in six minutes,
and believe you me,
it's a lot, you can
sail pretty far, nearly
to Byzantium in
six minutes, until
the rinky-dink
ship sputters
into port, until
other lovers get
strapped in, until
you get your
land legs back,
and still dizzy

beeline for
the closest roller
coaster, for the mad
teacup, for the Tilt-
A-Whirl, for those
bumper cars
of love we can’t
get enough of.

Nécessaire

Every Catherine
Deneuve has one.
Colette had two
toothbrushes in hers,
scissors, a clip-
on grin. French
women understand
what's essential,
what you need
to wake up
on the right
side of bedlam.
A pencil, an
eraser. Colette's
nécessaire was
small and blue—
a soupçon
of ocean you
could tie
your life
raft to.

Bridal

I didn't want
a wedding—
I wanted cake.
I didn't
want cake
so much
as I wanted
those figurines
atop sweet tiers.
I didn't want
the figurines, not
really. What I
wanted was
to be them—
hard and plastic,
machined
into being
with another,
as alive as
an ornament
can be,
on a sea
of buttercream,
someone maybe

taking a bite
out of me, someone
thinking I might
be real.

Message

I only folded my-
self, only slipped

inside this bottle
because I thought

there was a ship
in here, because

I thought you
might be on it.

Review

Sam, the bellman, was extremely helpful. We loved dining at the edge of the cliff. The woman who took our coats was very pleasant and promised to give them back. Our room had a window and an adjoining room. There were people above us, and we heard every sound they made. It sounded like happiness, and when we complained to the management, nothing happened. The bed was small, and it was hard to not remember the past. The television only played detective shows, episodes in which the main young character, a woman, fell off a cliff. Or jumped. It was never clear. There were too many menus to choose from. The terrace was above the sea. There was a jar of clouds. We could not reach it.

Circling

Someone was saying what
Oleg Gazenko said. No one

remembers who he was, but
they remember the name

of the dog he sent into space,
this Laika sent to fetch some

bone she couldn't bring back
since the technology for de-

orbiting didn't exist. We go
in circles—and toward what

end? Someone was quoting
Gazenko: *The more time passes,*

the more I am sorry. But what
I heard was, *the more I am*

afraid. Maybe sorrow and fear
aren't that different, maybe

they orbit each other, privy to
a similar whimpering that comes

when we go too far too
swiftly in this brittle dark.

Fable

I'm tired of meaning, says the tortoise
to the hare, who agrees. The lions

and crows don't disagree, and the snake
chimes in: it would be better if we didn't

have to moonlight as morality lessons.
Exactly, says the chicken. I'd like to

let loose once in a while, I'd like
to stretch my wings, she says.

Yes, says the fox. You should
get out of your pen more. You

should let me help, says the fox,
opening the latch to the evening.

It was a fine evening and a fine
conclusion they were coming to,

thought the fox, helping
the chicken out of her feathers.

Holding Pattern

People have been
detained for holding

unlit candles, for
wearing yellow

dresses, for possessing
umbrellas. It is, after all,

forbidden to mimic
a flower or threaten

the dark, and anyone
possessing anything

resembling a shield
will be confiscated.

The Dictator's Table

Pomegranates.
Map.
An eraser.
Peacock's feather.
Glass that's left
a red O
here and here
and here—
like a mouth
saying no,
no, no—

Alcatraz

How quickly one gets
from A to Z, how

swiftly one says
everything there

is to see: these
bars, for instance,

and the flexible
fencing of sharks,

and how impossibly
far it is—this

life from that.

Apples on a Chair

after Alvin Ross

There they are—three
apples on a white chair,

on a pillow on a chair,
where we have to imagine

they're comfortable,
where a sitter for a portrait

did not show, or was, by
a few luminous fruits,

upstaged. How will
we be remembered?

I am what I left—
pen, shell, the letter

I could not write.
Render that, with a grey

floor and ochre backdrop,
or better, rest a while

with apples on a pillow
on a small chair—

marvel at all
we call fallen.

Wading in Truro

You folded your clothes
neatly like someone
must have taught you,
then turned and walked
without stopping into
the winter water in those
ridiculous swim trunks
your wife would have rightly
called a disaster. It was a 40° sea
you were walking, then diving
into, a rain-grey morning you
surfaced to, yelling, *yes, yes, yes.*
Who were you talking to?
All the no's a life provides?
Or does breath, in overdrive,
make that sound without
thinking? Without having made
a real rescue plan, Tom and I,
onshore, watched. If he gets
into trouble, Tom said, I'll run in.
If you get into trouble, I told Tom,
can I have your stuff? Because
we all know how swiftly
things can go wrong

in water, and by the time
Tom hollered, *Come in*
already, you were already
numb, cradling your arms
as if someone had just
given them to you and you
weren't sure what arms
were for. They're for holding
stuff, Josh. They're for toweling
off, for feeling euphoric. They're
for holding a small dog in your lap,
as you did, as we sat afterwards
in a room snug with lamplight and fire.
We were drinking spiked cider.
We were talking about people
who fake their own deaths.
Who does that? you asked.
Only people who fake
their own lives, we decided.
And when I asked what
you were thinking, stripped
down, striding into the sea,
you said: *Nothing*. You said:
I was between thoughts, as

if between raindrops, while
Tom and I, who'd come,
ostensibly, as bodyguards
against the elements, just
gawked and marveled
at you and the waves—
how you went under, friend,
how you came back up.

Coming Back

for Jane Mead

I'd want to be
moss, she said—

moss, which greens
where grass can't—

a softness, a carpet
that doesn't fly

off, which isn't
magical, but

simply is
where

she isn't.

Roosevelt Dargon

Roosevelt Dargon, how often I have thought of you
and your leg. We were driving that last stretch
of slow road home, in snow and ice, in the blue
Vista Cruiser—what was I, five?—when your big
rig crashed. We didn't see it happen, but got there
right after, before the ambulance and cops, before
the snarl of cars that would have kept us from
reaching you. I say *us,* but what I mean is my father,
who told my brothers and me: *Stay here,* while my mother
toggled between static and Tommy Dorsey and he ran
to the jackknifed cab and found you pinned in there,
left leg mostly severed, but tethered enough under
the crushed front dash to keep several bigger men
from pulling you out. There was a lot of blood you
were losing, and the tumbled lumber and concrete
blocks from the load you'd been hauling, and the smashed
glass of cling peaches in syrup from the truck you'd
swerved into, and all around you fuel was pooling,
collecting, threatening to catch fire, and I have to imagine
what you would have heard: my father's voice, calm
and measured, saying, *I'm a doctor.* He might not have
said, *a psychiatrist.* What he showed you was
his Swiss Army knife, what he did was ask
permission to finish what the accident had started—

to cut the tendon, cleanly, to free you. I guess
we never know which part of ourselves we'll
have to sacrifice, or when we might need to say
to a stranger with a pocketknife: *I'd be obliged.*
And that was that. They pulled you out. Someone
may have grabbed the mangled leg as an after-
thought, but this was 1966, before the age
of reattachments. My father knelt in the snow
and wiped his knife blade clean. This was before
there would be people on the road we could
not help, before the next Christmas, and the ones
after that, when a crate of oranges would come
from Baltimore, with a card that said: *Best*
wishes from the leg and me, never specifying
which leg you meant—the one you kept
or the one you let go. What the mind
keeps, it keeps. I still have my mother
humming *I Thought About You,* still
have my brothers punching each other
in the wayback, still have my father,
still running with his Swiss
army, as if he could, in some
coming blizzard save us all.

Acknowledgments

The Arkansas International: “Review”

The Atlantic: “Ghosting,” “On Love”

The Best American Poetry: “Fable”

The Creative Process Arts & Literary Journal: “Losing My Religion”

Diode: “Independence Day, Arezzo”

Faultlines: “On Desire,” “Wading in Truro”

Glimpse: “Introduction to Color,“ “Message,” “Stretch”

The New York Review of Books: “Onions”

The New Yorker: “Roosevelt Dargon,” “Sugar”

Only Poems: “Spectacle,” “Habitat,” “Directive,” “Wax,” “Bridal,” “Contingency”

Pangyrus: “Coming Back”

Plume: “Safe,” “Tunnel”

Peripheries: “Apples on a Chair,” “Selfie Stick,” “Bio,” “Directional,” “My Father’s Watch”

Poetry: “Matinée,” “Fable”

Poetry London: “Circling”

Revel: “Nécessaire”

Terrain: “Clover,” “Dusk,” “Piecemeal,” “Shepherd,” “Those Red Hills”

The Threepenny Review: “Alcatraz,” “Holding Pattern”

Verse Daily: “Circling”

“Roosevelt Dargon” appears in *A Century of Poetry in The New Yorker: 1925–2025*

For heaping teaspoons, for sacks of the stuff, *thank you*: Razia Iqbal, Francesca Bewer, Amy Anderson, Giavanna Munafo, Gail Mazur, Robert Pinsky, Andy Senchak, Kiel Moe, Alice Sebold, Elizabeth Clubb, Tom Sleigh, Sarah Harwell, Josh Weiner, Sarah Blake, Ginny Threefoot, Olga Broumas, Danielle Jones, Sarah Keniston, Jean Wilcox, Bob Steinberg, Lise Motherwell, Melinda Mancini, the Allenbergs, Naomi Wallace, my brothers, and Bosco. And deep thanks to everyone at Four Way Books.

About the Author

Andrea Cohen's poems have appeared in *The New Yorker*, *The New York Review of Books*, *The Threepenny Review*, *The New Republic*, *The Atlantic Monthly*, and elsewhere. She is the author of nine poetry collections, including *Sugar*, *The Sorrow Apartments*, *Everything*, *Nightshade*, *Unfathoming*, *Furs Not Mine*, *Kentucky Derby*, *Long Division*, and *The Cartographer's Vacation*. Awards include a Guggenheim Fellowship and several residencies at MacDowell. She directs the Blacksmith House Poetry Series in Cambridge, MA.

Four Way Books is grateful to those individuals who participated in our Build a Book Program. They are:

Anonymous (10), Robert Abrams, Debra Allbery, Maggie Anderson, Kathy Aponick, Sally Ball, Jean Ball, Victor Basta, Adria Bernardi, Richard Blanchard, Laurel Blossom, adam b. bohannon, Lee Briccetti, Anthony Cappo, Anne Babson Carter, Cyrus Cassells, Jennifer Christman, Peter Coyote, Kwame Dawes, Michael Anna de Armas, Brian Komei Dempster, Patrick Donnelly, Lynn Emanuel, Joan Frank, Rigoberto González, Rachel Eliza Griffiths, Catherine Grossman, Naomi Guttman and Jonathan Mead, Beth Harrison, Jeffrey Harrison, KT Herr, Carlie Hoffman, Melissa Hotchkiss, Thomas and Autumn Howard, Parker Howe Foundation, Catherine Hoyser, Linda Susan Jackson, Elizabeth Jackson, Liz Janik, Marilyn Johnson, Deborah and Maria Jonas-Walsh, Elizabeth J. Kandall, Maeve Kinkead, Lindsay and John Landes, David Lee and Jamila Trindle, Rodney Terich Leonard, Howard Levy, Owen Lewis and Susan Ennis, Ralph and Mary Ann Lowen, Maja Lukic, Ricardo Alberto Maldonado, Donna Masini, Cleopatra Mathis, Lupe Mendez, Dale Neal, Mary Jane Nealon, Kathy Nelson, Marilyn Nelson, Nicole Nevadunsky, Kimberly Nunes, Rebecca and Daniel Okrent, Cathy McArthur Palermo, Marcia Pelletiere, Megan Pinto, Martha Rhodes, Paula Rhodes, Laurie Rosenblatt, Lyris Schonholz, Soraya Shalforoosh, Jennifer Skeele, Mary Slechta, Page Hill Starzinger, Sarah Stone, Yerra Sugarman, Marjorie and Lew Tesser, Reed Turchi, Maria Walsh, Martha Webster and Robert Fuentes, Calvin Wei, George Whalen Jr., Mark Wunderlich, Kathleen Zimmerman, and Carol Zoref.